Contents

Some words are shown in bold, **like this**. You can find out what they mean by looking in the glossary.

What is the environment?

The environment is the air, water, and land all around us. People depend on the environment. We need:

- water for drinking, cooking, and washing
- air to breathe
- land to live on and to grow plants on for food.

People can damage the environment. They can **pollute** water and air. They can cut down forests and clear areas of countryside. People can also spoil the environment when they drop litter.

When people damage the environment they hurt themselves and other living things. For example, animals may get tangled in litter or choke on it. When people cut down trees, animals that lived in or fed from the trees suffer.

Why do people cut down trees?

CLUE

- How could people use the land?

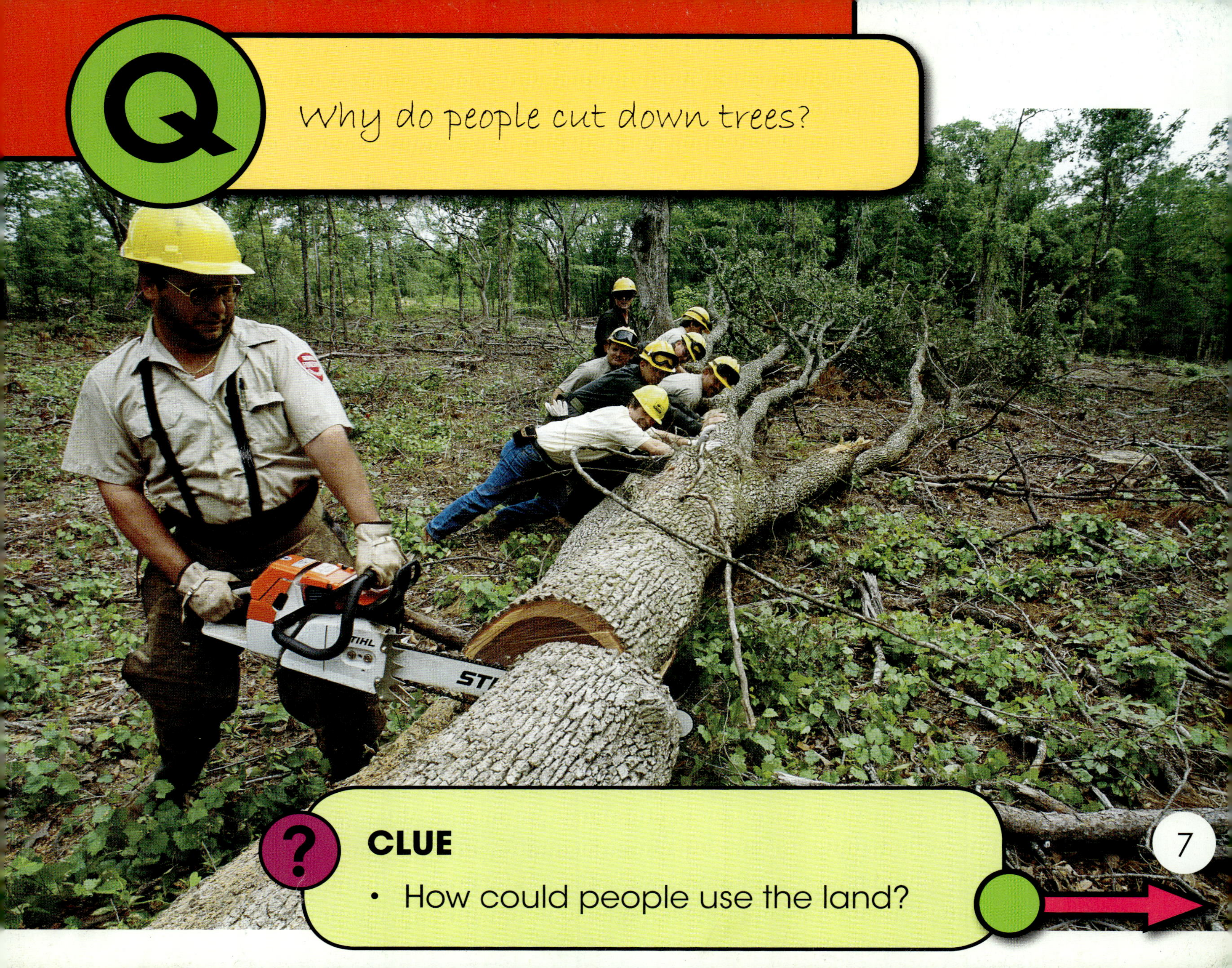

A

People cut down trees to clear land. They use the land for building houses, supermarkets, roads, and other things. They also use the land for farming.

The way people get rid of waste affects the environment, too. Most waste is taken to huge dumps called **landfills**. These use large areas of countryside. Waste can create nasty liquids and gases. These **pollute** the ground, water, and the air.

Water pollution

These are some of the ways people **pollute** lakes, rivers, and seas.

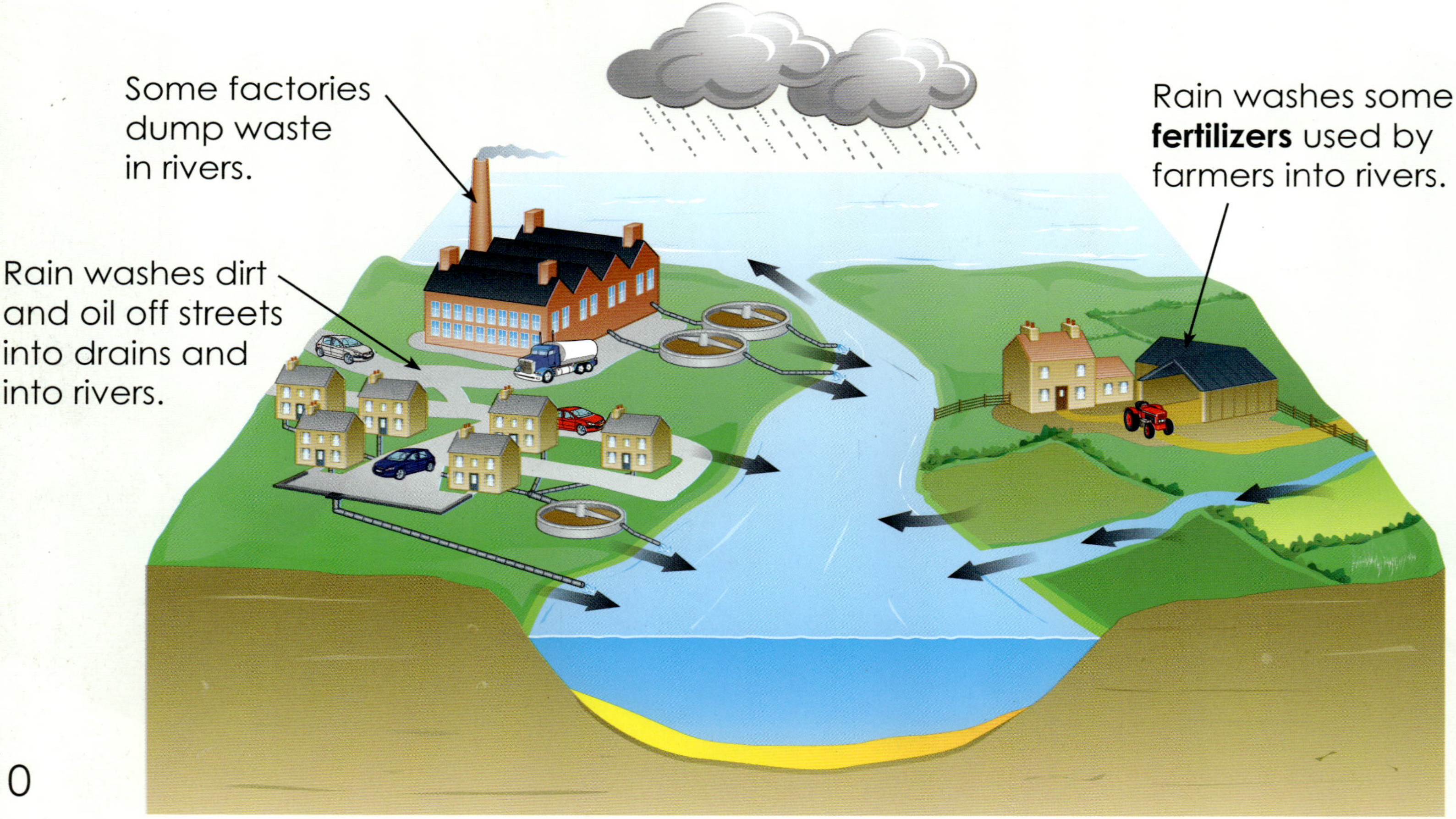
Some factories dump waste in rivers.
Rain washes dirt and oil off streets into drains and into rivers.
Rain washes some **fertilizers** used by farmers into rivers.

How does water pollution hurt people and other living things?

CLUES

- Can people drink dirty water?
- Do animals live in water?

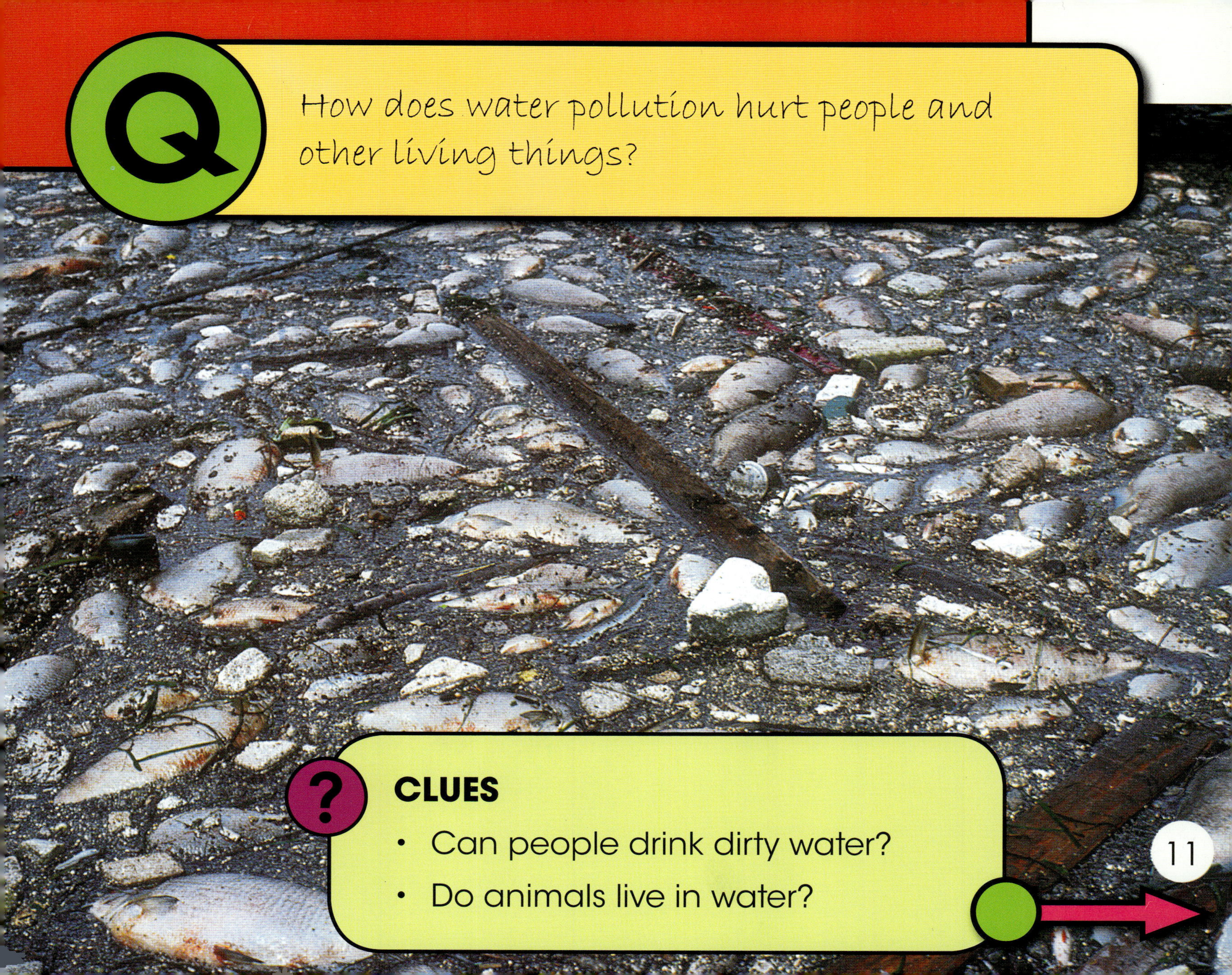

A

Dirty water can kill wildlife such as fish. Dirty water makes people ill if they drink it. When water is **polluted** there is less clean water for people to use.

These people have to queue to collect the clean water they need to live.

When **fertilizer** from farms washes into streams, it feeds **algae** that grow quickly. When the algae die, **bacteria** help to rot them. The bacteria use up oxygen (air) from the water. Then there is not enough oxygen left for other water plants and fish, so they die.

Air pollution

When people burn fuels like coal, gas, or oil they release gases such as **carbon dioxide** into the air. In power stations, people burn fuel to make electricity. People use electricity to light and heat their homes. Electricity makes machines like televisions and computers work.

↑ Most power stations and factories **pollute** the air. The gas they make by burning fuel escapes into the air and causes air pollution.

Cars, planes, and other vehicles work by burning fuel, too. People use vehicles for travelling and to transport food and other goods. Vehicles also make air pollution. Air pollution makes people cough and can give them breathing problems.

Some people need inhalers like this to help them breathe.

Global warming

There is a layer of gases all around Earth. It keeps our planet warm. Without these "**greenhouse gases**" it would be too cold for us to live on Earth. Like the glass in a greenhouse, the gases keep it warmer inside than out!

This is how greenhouse gases trap the Sun's heat on the Earth.

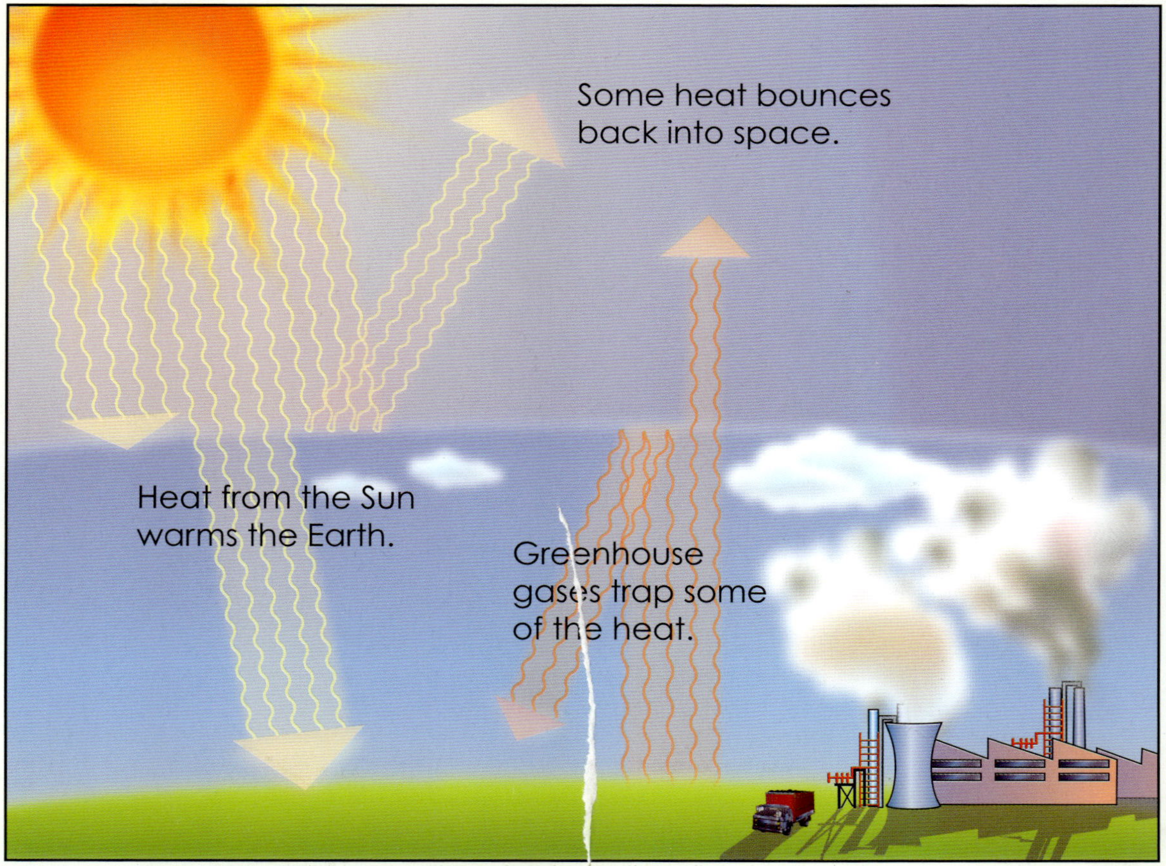

Some heat bounces back into space.
Heat from the Sun warms the Earth.
Greenhouse gases trap some of the heat.

Q

When people burn fuel in vehicles, factories, and power stations it makes greenhouse gases. What do you think happens when people burn more and more fuel?

CLUE

- What would happen if greenhouse glass were thicker?

A

Burning more fuel makes more **greenhouse gases**. More gases trap more heat around the Earth. This makes the average temperatures on Earth higher. This is called **global warming**.

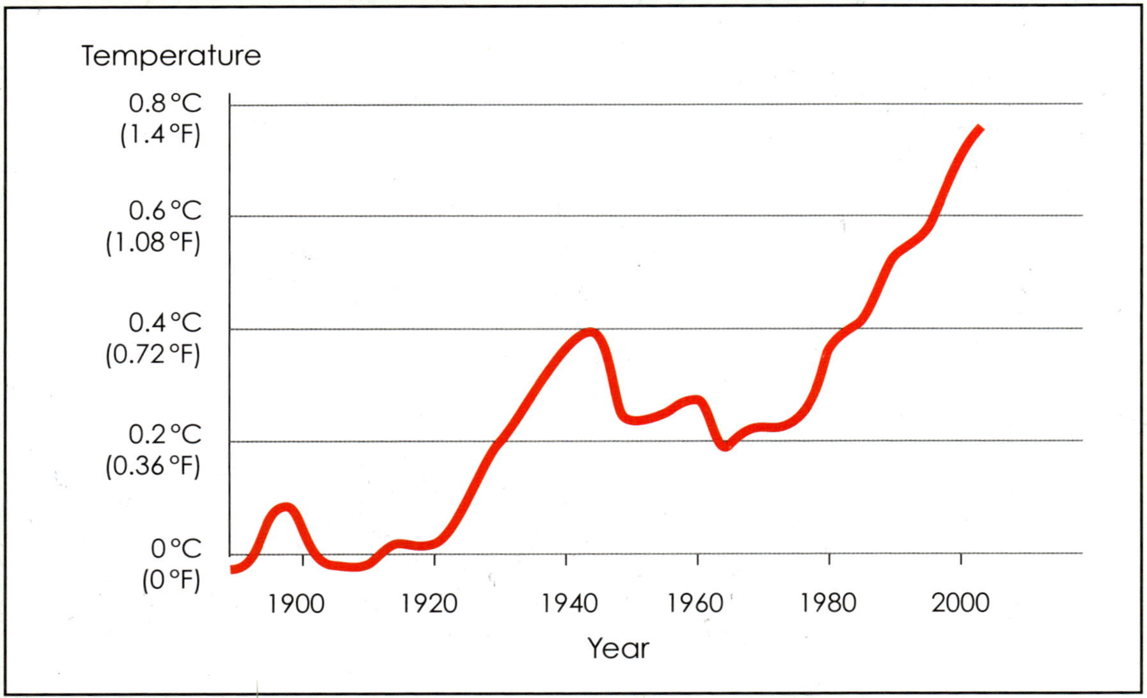

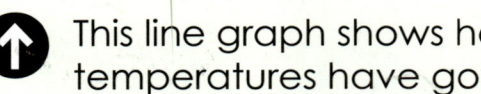

This line graph shows how average world temperatures have got warmer since 1850. This is when people started to use machines and vehicles.

Global warming is making the ice at the North Pole and South Pole melt. When this ice melts, there is more water in the oceans and they rise. Many islands and coasts may be under water in future.

↑ As ice melts, polar bears have further to swim to find food. Many get tired and drown.

Caring for the environment

People need to care for the environment to keep it safe. To protect the environment people should:

- reduce: use less and buy less
- reuse: keep things to use in different ways
- recycle: change waste into things we can use again.

We can also care for the environment by clearing up litter.

Q How can people use less fuel?

CLUE

- How do you get to school?

A

People can use less fuel by walking, cycling, or sharing lifts to get around.

When people leave the car at home they put less **carbon dioxide** into the air. It is better to travel by bus or train instead. Walking and cycling also keep you fit!

People can reduce the amount of electricity they use by:

- turning off the television, computers, and lights when they leave a room
- turning down the heating and putting jumpers on instead
- using low-energy light bulbs.

Reusing things is easy, too. You could mend a pair of jeans rather than buy a new pair. You could borrow books and DVDs from the library instead of buying new ones. You could buy second-hand clothes at charity shops or jumble sales instead of new ones.

You can reuse jars by storing things in them.

What kinds of packaging can be recycled?

CLUE

- Can anything in these pictures be recycled?

A

Card, glass, metal cans, and some plastics can be recycled and made into new things.

Plastic bottles can be shredded, melted down, and remade into pens, fleece jackets, and even shoes!

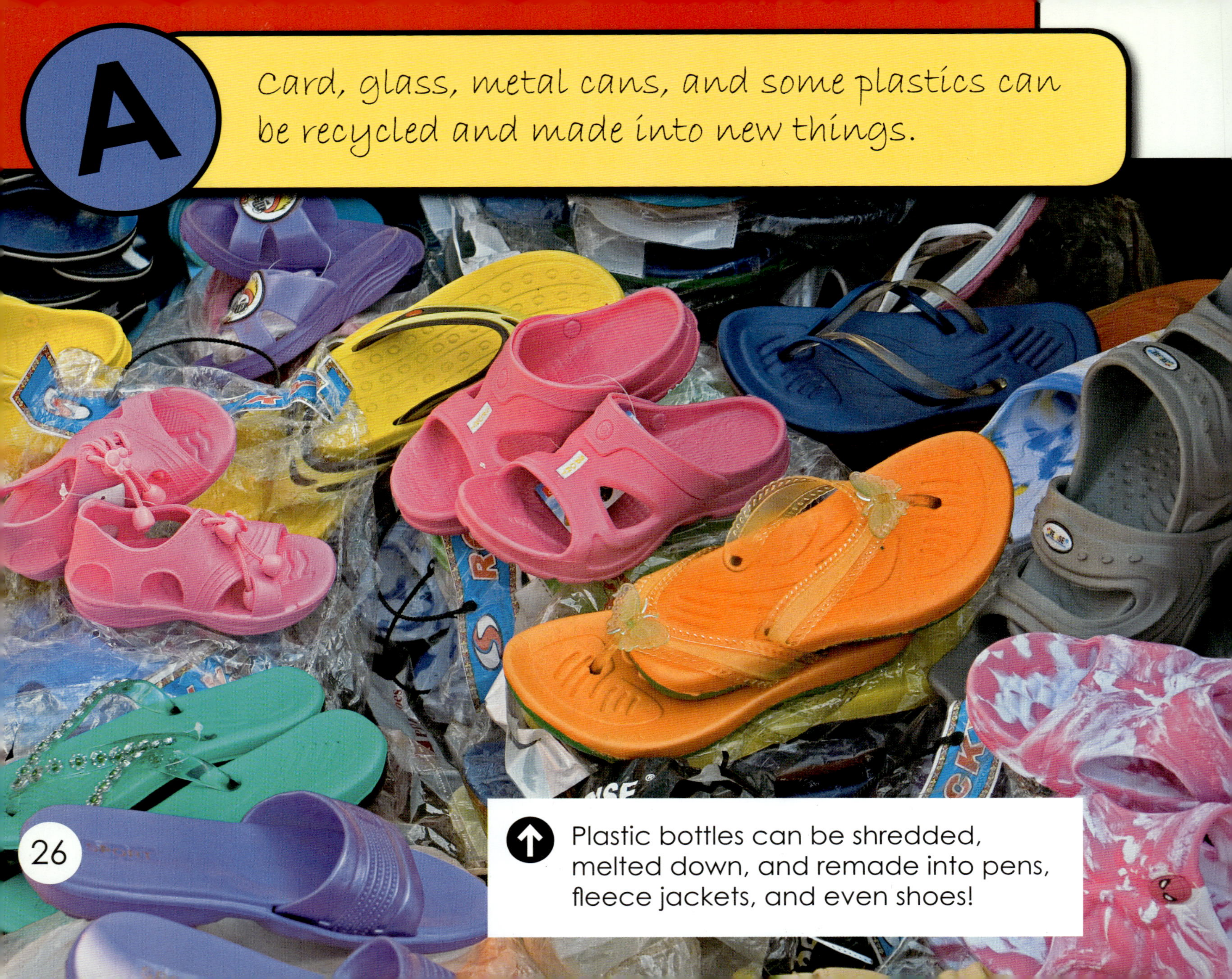

People can damage the environment when they dig up or take materials from the Earth. To get the metal to make 1 tonne of drinks cans, miners dig up 5 tonnes of rock. When people make recycled cans they need no new metal.

We can recycle food waste like apple cores, too. In a **compost heap**, food waste slowly rots and becomes a brown, crumbly mixture. When people put compost on gardens and fields, **nutrients** from the food waste help plants grow.

This chart shows the different kinds of waste you might find in many people's dustbins. People could reduce this waste by at least two-thirds if they reduced, reused, and recycled.

If we all make an effort to waste less, we can help to protect the environment for the future.

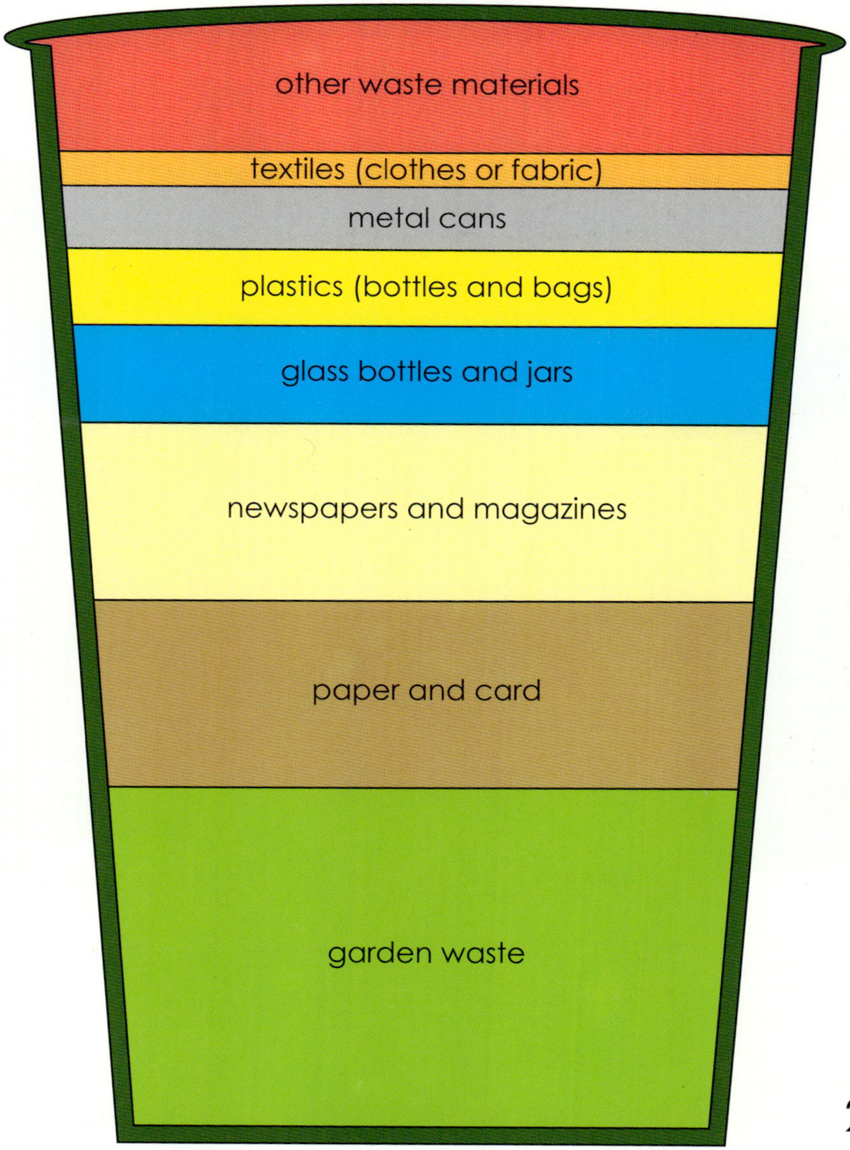

Checklist

People can damage the environment when:

- they **pollute** water and air
- they cut down forests and clear areas of countryside
- they drop litter.

We can protect the environment by:

reducing

reusing

recycling

Glossary

algae plant-like living things

bacteria living things so small we cannot see them. Some bacteria cause diseases.

carbon dioxide gas that people release into the air when they burn fuel in cars, factories, and power stations

compost heap heap of plant and food waste that rots down to form compost. People put compost in the soil to help plants grow.

fertilizer powders, sprays, or liquids that farmers put on soil to help plants grow

global warming increase in average world temperatures

greenhouse gas gas that traps heat around the Earth, such as carbon dioxide

landfill site where waste is dumped in a big hole and covered with soil

nutrient substance that is important for a living thing's health

pollute when smoke, gases, or other substances damage the air, soil, or water

Index